The Yin and Yang of Marriage

Survival lessons from more
than 30 years together.

Stephanie Ager Kirz
Howard L. Kirz, M.D.

This little book was written by my late
husband and me as a wedding gift for my sister
Mary Liz Ager's marriage in 2002. We patterned
it after a "he said, she said" format so our
separate Yin and Yang voices, which made our
marriage strong, could be heard. She encouraged
me to publish these lessons to share with others
since I was fortunate to have spent 36 incredible
years with my wonderful husband Howard Kirz
who died tragically of an instant heart attack
in 2008. I was very blessed to have had such a
loving marriage that lasted so many years.

It is with great love and gratitude that I dedicate
these lessons to all couples who are working on
their own special relationship.

I encourage you to pass along your own words of
wisdom in the last chapter of this book.

~ Stephanie

CONTENTS

1. Shared Activities

One of the most essential things about our relationship is that we've always spent a lot of time together, sharing interests and activities like friends. In the early days when we were both working 60-hour weeks we'd spend the weekends together. Sometimes we'd go hiking or backpacking, hunting for antiques, checking out a county fair or heading off on various short trips around the Northwest.

As we've gotten older our shared activities have changed. Since our joints are stiffer these days we bike more, take planes more, go to more plays and restaurants and sometimes we just hang around and read the Sunday paper together. In our twentieth year we took fourteen months off and hung out in Southern France. We used to say we did it to "rebuild our marriage bankroll." Today we make dates with each other to go to movies and try out new restaurants. It seems to me that it's not so much the activities themselves that have worked for us, but the fact that we've always explored our world together and hence have learned and grown together. We started out as good friends a long time ago. Thirty years (and a lot of margaritas) later...we still are. *HLK*

..... and Separate Activities

On the other hand we don't try to do everything together. God forbid! Here's an insider's tip: free, unsupervised time is a secret to success. I've always had my own hobbies, my own special projects. Good heavens, Howard wouldn't know a retrograde Mercury from a conjunct Mars and Saturn. He doesn't like tennis and I think fishing is dumb. But Howard's always wondering what I'm up to and I think that's part of what keeps him interested. Maybe the same is true for me. Mostly we're wondering, when the other one is wandering off, what kind of trouble they'll be getting into. And who knows what it will be, but it's always fun, and it keeps us on our toes. *SAK*

II. Joint Finances

They say family finances are one of the things that drive couples apart. I learned that from my mom and dad. From the beginning Stephie and I have talked about our mutual finances. April (tax time) is one month every year when we're sure to do this. We talk about how much we've earned (or not), how much we've saved (or not) and what financial plans we have for the coming year. Most of the time we do an annual budget together and since we keep separate checkbooks (see below), we decide who's going to pay for what, who's going to save what and so on. Over thirty years each of us has had periods when our careers and earnings have been stormy. We've learned that just keeping an open discussion between us on our long term financial picture allows us both to feel like we're on the same financial ship. That way we keep cruising along together, regardless of the financial weather. *HLK*

..... and Separate Finances

But separate personal checkbooks. Definitely! In fact, in 30 years Howard has never once seen my checkbook. And, he'd probably pass out if he did because I never keep a balance. Occasionally I call the 1 800 number and get the automated balance just to make sure that things are ok. I have a personal relationship with a very sweet banker who keeps me out of trouble. Howard has never even met her. Plus, I don't think he really wants to know how much I actually spend on the dog or doing my hair or those late night calls to the astrologer. Joint finances, but separate checkbooks, that's the secret. *SAK*

III. Joint space

Somebody once said to me that their home was
their sanctuary. I wondered what that meant.
When I was working long hours, home to me
was just dust balls, an empty refrigerator and
a very rare cleaning. Now that I'm older and
have more time, my home is a place where I
can create a comfortable nest for the two of us.
A love nest. A place to be quiet, a reflection
of our acquired tastes, our travels, joint and
separate interests and lifestyle. It's a fun place to
share with friends who appreciate the magical
setting and an occasional sunset. Our home is
a collaboration of our shared vision of who we
are and how we choose to live. *SAK*

..... and Separate Space

Hah. The only thing wrong with her description is that she's a natural born pig! It may be that our shared space is a collaboration etc etc but the thing I personally value most is my separate space. Ever since we lived in a teeny house in Leschi we've preserved some separate space for each of us, at least a separate desk. Personally I like the basement and the garage. Stephie's spaces (e.g. the office and computer on which she's writing her part of this) are way too messy for me. I don't want to clean them, I don't want her to clean them, I just don't want to have to look at them. So today even in our retirement years we still have two separate offices and two separate computers. I never, never look into Stephie's space, and if she hadn't hung the sign "No boys allowed" on her door I'd have put one up myself. Thank God for doors. *HLK*

IV. Health

As an Emergency Physician I saw a lot of
death. Never met anybody who actually
thought they were going to die, at least not
on the day they did. It gives you a really
acute sense of both the fragility of life and the
importance of maintaining the best health
you can. We've always been fairly conscious
of the importance of keeping our bodies
working well. Reasonable diets (booze is good
for you), exercise and relaxation have been
a part of our marriage. Neither of us seems
to be able to keep it up by ourselves. Both of
us do our part. As we've gotten older various
injuries and illnesses have accumulated and
we've succumbed to the occasional pharmacy
or doctor, but we still remind each other of
the need to watch our weight and floss our
teeth and we probably both hope it'll give us
more good years together. If not, we'll just be
stretching together in the next life. *HLK*

..... and Sickness

It's funny but you never think about the bad times when things are going well. But part of being together is sharing the times when things aren't going right. Like when you're blue or when you're sick. So that's really part of it, being supportive, being a friend in need. When Howard broke his back bicycling, it took the two of us three years, as a team, to get him back on track. When I had stomach trouble he held my hand and kissed me while they were passing the endoscope. In some ways, you need to spend more time with the other person when they're not feeling well than when they're healthy. Well, you know what I mean. *SAK*

V. Sex

Sex is good for you. Sex is healthy. Better even than flossing. Sex is what you think about day and night when you're first together. Once I made Stephie a badge for being "The World's Fastest Undresser". (Remember our deal "No editing what the other one writes!") Over time it's important to try different places and different kinds of sex. You know "keep it interesting" or something like that. Some of my fondest travel memories include a rock in Castle Craigs and a bathroom in Banff. Wonder if anybody's ever published a guide to those kinds of things? *HLK*

..... and More Sex

Need we say more? There are lots of kinds
of sex. Cuddling in the morning, kissing
in the car, quickies in the woods, holding
hands in the movies, making a big mess
in hotels. They're all important. It's
biology.....and it's in the stars. *SAK*

VI. Friends

Friends are the angels who dance with you on the stages of your life. Our separate friends help us maintain a sense of who we are as individuals and our mutual friends join us in experiencing life as a couple. Some friends fish and some friends do bars, some play tennis and some smoke cigars. They're all important to maintaining a connection with the world around us. Friends are counselors and confidants. We think a wide circle of them is critical to a strong marriage. *HLK*

..... and Foes

On the other hand friends are like chameleons.
They can change color on you. Sometimes
they're right for one setting and just terrible in
another. And some people are just plain bad to
begin with. It's important to help protect your
partner from the bad people, and some who say
they're friends but really aren't. And it can be
hard to tell the difference. A second sense will
often help your sweetie realize what's really going
on. Listen to them. Protecting yourself and
your sweetie from bad folks is almost as useful as
spending time with the good ones. *SAK*

VII. Family

Every marriage comes with family. Various combinations: parents, step parents, brothers, sisters, step brothers, step sisters, cousins, aunts, uncles, children, grandchildren etc. The person who said "You can choose your friends but not your family" was dead on. Good family members help celebrate life's events and can be amongst the greatest friends and greatest loves of our lives. Some of them. But never all of them. The key is to sort it out. You can't change your family members or even choose them, but you can enjoy the relationships that work for you and ignore the rest. The key is getting a handle on your own behavior, not worrying about theirs. *HLK*

..... and No Family

Someone once said to me, "Why do I need friends, I have my family?" This was not a well person. It's important to remember that when you were little, you needed love, support and approval from your family. It's not as important when you get older. Nice, yes. But not necessary. You're not married to your family or your partner's family. You marry one another. At the end of the day, the person you can count on is the person standing by your side. It's their love, approval and support that you really need. *SAK*

VIII. Respect

Each person brings a whole different set of skills and perspectives to a relationship. At least that's our experience. I have no ability to spend more than 10 minutes in the left-brain, analytic zone. Howard, on the other hand, can easily spend hours there and then quickly switch to his right-brain side. I love that about him. In turn he calls me a creative dyslexic. Sometimes I just see things in completely illogical but much more interesting ways. He loves that about me. We respect and love these sorts of differences. It's the differences that add pizzazz to our relationship. Our mutual respect has grown from understanding that one truth. *SAK*

..... and Disrespect

On the other hand it's not necessary to like everything about your partner. There are times when disagreements are critical to expressing your emotions or finding a solution. Life in my family was one long argument. We yelled at breakfast but found common ground by lunch. Raising your voice in Stephie's family was considered unbecoming. They smiled a lot. So when we were first together I would yell and Stephie would cry. Not too functional huh? One day we both realized the problem and she asked me to explain how you could express anger and not destroy the relationship. Since she was pretty soft spoken then I just showed her how to slam doors. BLAM, BLAM, BLAM! Once she got it she slammed the basement door off its hinges. She's stopped slamming doors for some time now, but boy can she yell. *HLK*

IX. Communication

"It's not what you say that counts, its what you don't say." Well, it's also what you say. So what does that mean? It means you have to take time to talk and to listen and you need to ask what the other person is feeling and then ask what they're thinking. Because that's two different things. We're not mind readers. Although I suspect Howard is actually psychic, he still can't always tell what I'm thinking. And vice versa. Sometimes he just grunts and I haven't a clue what that means. So we talk. And then we talk some more. And some more. And in the end, we understand each other and ourselves better. I guess that's communication. *SAK*

..... and Silence

I've never had any trouble with the talking part and I'm not too bad at listening but living with Stephie has taught me a third part, the value of silence. I have an opinion about everything (mostly), but over the years I've learned that it's not always necessary to share it. One time she pranced up the sidewalk with very very black hair. I looked out the window and chirped "What happened to you, did they make a mistake?" These days when her roots are showing or the fat over her knees is jiggling I just smile. When she's distressed about something I don't always offer a fix in the first ten seconds; I just thank her "for sharing" or say "I know how you feel." Silence, thirty years of marriage has taught me, is a golden part of communication too. *HLK*

X. Love

I still don't know the meaning of Love.
All I know is that after 30 years, I smile
and my heart still melts whenever I see my
sweetie. Is it chemistry? Is it biology? Is it
communication? Respect? Is it growing
together over the years? I don't know.

Maybe it's all the above......and a whole
lot of luck. *SAK*

..... and More Love

Me too. I still look forward to the sound of her heels clicking just around the corner and the sweet sight of her face on my pillow. *HLK*

We're not sure what it is or what makes it happen but we are sure we wish you all the very best of luck and much much love on your own grand adventure.

Blessings,
Stephanie - *SAK*
&
Howard - *HLK*

XII. Your Own
Words of Wisdom

*"There is no greater gift
than the gift of love."*

~ Steven Wilde

www.ingramcontent.com/pod-product-compliance
Lightning Source LLC
Chambersburg PA
CBHW060559030426
42337CB00019B/3574